T0149427

The Black Suit

Written by
Carlos Antonio Baca

Edited by
Janel M. Keller

Cover Illustration by
Christopher L. Casanovas

iUniverse, Inc.
New York   Bloomington

Black Suit

iUniverse books may be ordered through booksellers or by contacting:

iUniverse
1663 Liberty Drive
Bloomington, IN 47403
www.iuniverse.com
1-800-Authors (1-800-288-4677)

Because of the dynamic nature of the Internet, any Web addresses or
links contained in this book may have changed since publication and
may no longer be valid. The views expressed in this work are solely those
of the author and do not necessarily reflect the views of the publisher,
and the publisher hereby disclaims any responsibility for them.

ISBN: 978-1-4401-2621-5 (pbk)
ISBN: 978-1-4401-2622-2 (ebk)

Printed in the United States of America

iUniverse rev. date: 3/5/2009

I dedicate this book to all the lost souls in the world. I just want to tell you that I've been there and I know what you are going through. I hope this book helps at least one person.

Acknowledgements

I'm eternally grateful for all the loved ones in my life, but I have to thank all the people that inspired me to write this book, especially one in particular that without her this book would be non-existent. I would like to thank my family for their support and understanding. I thank all my friends that believed in me and spent time helping me with this project. My editor and my good friend Janel, without you I know I could not have done this. To Chris my brother, I knew I picked the right person to draw this cover. To Gigi and Susie you girls are the light in my life. Michael and Brandon my best friends, a person could not ask for better friends than you guys. Finally to all that chose to pick up this book and let me in their lives I thank you from the bottom of my heart.

The Recap

Two years ago there were two of me
One blinded and misguided
The other screaming to wake up
My fiancé cheating on me
All the signs clear to him
Have you ever loved someone so much
That when this is done your heart is gone?
Gone like the dreams and hope of a forgotten time
Time you will never get back
Back to past you can never go
Go because all it is left is the carcass of that love
The remains of betrayal and a false love
So with my heart growing cold I left
The procedure was long and damaging for all
Sank into a world that comforted me
A me, which only I could have helped
Her lies to her were unseen
Always undermining my intelligence
Encouragement never around

This is the recap of stories told and foretold
So many people warning me
It happened once, it will repeat itself
How right were those, but its okay
Mistakes are done
Done are the lessons of a misguided love

A year I lived in the wrong
Mistaken decisions I made
Treating women like I never have
I lost myself in the wrongs of the world
The good finish last was my anthem
The anthem only the weak speak of

1

Of those ladies an angel aroused
Rose to help man in distress
The emergency number was dialed for my soul
The light was diminishing in my eyes
My eyes full of misery and apathy
Empathy is what I was shown
The light was shown to me but months I took to embrace
Embrace all that were close to me
Even in my destruction my friends were shown
Those shown were my salvation
The angel disappeared because of me
The journey taught all I know
I walk a fine line seen by none
Reality and truth was the product of all this
Navigated Chaos and spit in its face
I even turned my back on God
Cursing Him for my pain, not thanking for my gifts
Later I understood my plan
Even the good turn bad
I'm back to do good

Time has come to end this recap of my life
I concentrate on my life now
Always hoping the woman of my life appears
The one the comforts me with a hug
Says nothing yet says everything
Unselfish in her actions
Only then can I give my all again
While I wait I write to all
For everyone that wants to read and hear
Bearing my trials of life
Writing not what I want but what is meant to be told
Coming so far from the past
Even a gift was presented to her

These thoughts I leave with
Love is the forgotten jewel
The lost golden chalice of life
Everything else can be obtained
Only love is given

Stage One

"Simple Beginnings"

A Summer of My Life

It started with a sad goodbye
A love I never had
My summer started with a shot to the heart
But I asked myself what heart?
If it was never filled
The blame is on me
Not only did she leave, but I did nothing
She left without me being able to do anything
Her images became a torment
I couldn't sleep, all I did was cry
We weren't a couple, we were just friends
Maybe that was it
If I had never known how wonderful and perfect she was,
I wouldn't have cried so much
I saw her twice that summer
Both ended with failed attempts
I adored her
I loved her
But maybe it was for the best
If I would have told her
But what if she would have said no
There would be no more hope
My heart would have been even more broken
But what if she had said yes
Then I lost the chance and now I suffer
I hope she is happy
I hope she is well
I'll be fine

The Rain

After my heart was broken
I began to cry
After the season of happiness
The rainy season came
This rain I feel inside of me
Like acid, destroying me from within
My soul drowning in my pain
The rain came after my happiness
Destroying everything in me
Everything good
Now turning it into pain
The rain does not stop
But I want it to
To fill my soul
Feel complete again
This is my simple wish

A New Page

A new page has turned in my life
Full of laughter and love
New sensations I have never felt
All because of love
A love greater than life itself
A new me has been born
From peasant to king
She is my queen and I am her king
Together we reign

To be with her for eternity and more
To love her
As she loves me.
Drawing me out of loneliness
Changing my writing, from dark to light
Taking care of me
She is there
Relationships come and go
Love is what stays
And she is staying with me

The wait was worth it, love at such a young age
A woman so wonderful, even more than I could ever dream
She is the one that changed me
For her I would give it all
For her I am changing
I am not perfect, but she is.

My Love

I think you must know,
You must know that I love you
I don't think you know how much

Without you, I'm not here
Without your love I'm lost
You guide me in life
Before you, I was confused
What to do, why, when, how?
Your light shined and cleared my horizon
No more clouds in my mind

My love, each time I see you I jump
I gasp for air when I see you
So beautiful you are
My love, words cannot describe you
My words do not even come close
They cannot capture you
But you are so captivating
My love...
Two words I'm honored to say

Things I Love About You

I love when you smile
I love when you tell me you love me
I love gazing upon you
I love your lips
I love when they meet mine
I love your passion
I love those deep eyes I lose myself in
I love dreaming with you
I love when I'm with you
I love the feeling I have the instant I see you
I love hearing your voice
I love those dimples
I love your warmth
I love how you turn bad into good
I love when you caress my face
Most of all I love you for being you
The Queen of my heart

Four

Four is a number
But no mere number it is
Four is special
As special as you and I

It was four months I knew I loved you
Four rings, for you to answer my first call
Four tries just to kiss you
But none to hug you

Four hours in a movie, never happened to us
Titanic would of been the one, but sorry I had to return it on time
For the start of a conversation, it never starts at four
But four always ends it all
Four periods of ten minutes is our short good-bye
Imagine a long one, four hours at least

Four seasons have passed to make it one year
I cannot wait sixteen seasons so four years could come
Every number is special, but none like four
The 4th of July is important, but January 4th is for us
The 3rd was no good
I broke my watch
Its alright it had a four year warranty
The fourth came, I asked you out

I have to go
Its almost 4th period

I Need You

I need you when I'm cold
I need you when I'm not strong
I need the warmth you give

You are the sun and the brightest star to me
Your rays when they touch, just keep me warm
When you pass by me, it's like a cool summer breeze
Your smile
It is like the sun shinning the most to please me
Your breath
The nicest breeze on a summer night
Your kiss
The finest and most refreshing cup of water,
Stopping my thirst for you
Your hug
My blanket in the night to cover me from any deadly chills

I need you to keep me alive

Metaphorically Speaking

You are the one
My true love
If loving you is crazy
Then I am in an asylum
If loving you is a crime
Then I'm guilty, put me away

Loving you is the greatest feeling
As wonderful as light mist gently setting on my face
A treasure so wonderful
A bright star guiding my life
You are my better half
Without you there is no me
I can't imagine a world of mine without you
Even if I can I shall not, it is too sad

Metaphorically speaking
If you are a carpenter
I would be a piece of wood
If you were the moon
I would gladly be the ocean
I look at the sky a piece is missing
The slice of heaven that you are

What a lucky man I am
Next to my celestial queen
My beautiful, kind-hearted lady of love
I love you with all my heart

Stage Two

"Things of the Mind"

Memories

Memories
Never leave
They are always present
They come when least expected
Painful or painless
As clear as ever
Yet they happened some time ago

Memories
Making us re-live something that happened a long time ago
Doesn't matter if it was painful
Making past decisions seem doubtful
Making a person re-think
Triggered or not, they come
Images flash before your eyes
Before realizing, they are gone
Leaving the pain or the joy
Memories are our link to our past
Memories are part of our souls

Memories of Love

They are all lies
They can't be forgotten
No matter how many times we tell ourselves
Once you love someone
Part of your heart is gone with them

When you loved someone
You cannot just stop caring
Is it human nature to care so much?
Time and distance could be a solution
But when you see your past love again
You cannot help but care

Once love comes back
The past love will no longer be your love
Maybe love is the solution to forget love
You can stop loving your old love
But you can never forget one thing
Memories always stay

Love to Me

Love is the most powerful force
Love is also fragile
One bend and it could snap

Love is for everyone
Everyone deserves to be loved
Everyone is capable of loving
But just because you deserve love,
Does not mean you are going to get it.

Love is wanted by everyone
Some are so desperate for love
They confuse it for other feelings
That is what I would call a mistake

Some are so afraid of it,
They will make excuses not to love
Some just cannot see love when it is in front of them

Just remember
There is no such thing as a perfect person
Only a person perfect for you
And you should never give up
If you do, you will miss what could be your happiest
moments.
If you have found love, do not let it go
If you have not found it yet
Keep looking, it is out there.

That is love to me.

The Other

Stuck between two
Two not of the same kind
One my perfect fit
The other with the flaws I want
One I have but temptations always creep
I have one but I want the other too
To feel the other's luscious lips
But to let go of the warmth of hers
What to do?
What is right, what's wrong?
Hold on or let loose?
One is calm, the other is wild
One is modest, the other is loud
I love one, but do I love the other too?
One is mine
The other can be mine
I don't know what to do.

Dream

A fall of never ending length
Everything is dark
As you fall, the wind feels like it's tearing your face apart
Just before the end, it stops
Eyes open, you find yourself levitating above the ground
It's making sure you see your fate
Then suddenly it drops you again
When you hit the ground;
Your eyes open, out of breath, sweating
Finding yourself in your bed
It was a nightmare

You find yourself living your fantasy
Where happiness never seems to go away
On the outside you smile
Never ending happiness abruptly disturbed by a noise
This noise is becoming louder
As you find the source, you hit it and everything turns black
Light suddenly appears again as you open you eyes,
It was just a nice dream

The Problem

I do not want to forget
But it hurts not to
The pain is engulfing me, please aid me
This is all I have
My problem is that I like it

Everything spins, I'm so confused
How can I get her out?
I need to forget
I don't even have her
And I can't forget
She is so far, but the distance is not the issue
The issue on hand is to forget her presence
Her essence must get out of me
Once again I'll try

My problem is I won't forget her
My problem is she's not mine
My problem is her beauty, I have to forget her
How can I forget the unforgettable?
How to forget that night
A night of remembering
How can something so right, be wrong?
But wrong it was

My problem is I cannot forget
She lured me and played me for a fool
But I still picture her with me
I can't help it, I regret it
Maybe this will aid

Stage Three

"A Lasting Relationship"

We Belong Together

At first a fling
Then constantly calling
Grew to caring
And finally to love

Ever since the first time I laid my eyes on you
Since that first phone call
I knew you were the one for me

I remember our dates
We talked for hours
I recall 9 o' clock we had to stop
But we snuck some extra time just to talk

Through thick and thin
Passed every obstacle
We had our fights,
But we also had our make-ups

We belong together
Our hands fit perfectly
Our thoughts are mirror images
Our ways clash at times
But when mixed it is perfection

Both stubborn
Both right all the time
But one always gives up
When it comes to us, we both agree

I drive you crazy
So crazy must be a disease
Two crazy love birds
We belong together

I Write

I write and write
All of it is for you
Everything I write is for you, about you, being with you
Poems, songs, stories
Of our love, our feelings
My feelings towards you

You mesmerize me with your beauty
And I write...
I write how you changed my life
How I cannot live without you
My energy comes from you
This I write

I write about how I picture our future
How I look at you
How I feel when you pass your hands through mine
I will keep writing about you and I
This I write, testify and put it in stone.

The Power

Throughout my life I tried
To find absolute power
To find absolute love
I thought they were two different things
But they are one in the same.

Absolute love is absolute power
The heart's will is powerful
This power is great between two people
Without it I cowered before obstacles
Not anymore

My mind tells me to leave and let her be fine
My heart says don't let love and happiness go
You are what she wants and loves, it will hurt her
Before my mind guided me, no more

This power will guide me
The power of the heart
The power of love
The power of our love

I will not let you go
When you are weakening
I will give you the strength you need
I would give my all to save you
I give you my vow of love
I will not let you go, I will be here
This I promise you
This love I will not let go, I will not surrender
The power of our love will survive

I imagine us happy at last
Without worrying about anything
Passing our love to the young
Showing the power of love overcomes anything
You just have to believe

If you believe you will be guided
And happiness will come
Don't fight it, just go
With love everything is possible

The question is do you believe in this?
Because if you do, everything will fall in place
Peace and tranquility will come
Love will be victorious.

Restrained

I feel like a scorpion in a ring of fire
Like a mouse in a mouse trap
Like a person on house arrest
I feel restrained

I feel asphyxiated without your love
I can't see you much and I want to
Each time I do, it brings pain
The pain of not seeing you again

I feel worn down
Without energy to keep you happy
Without money
Restrained
I can't take you to all the places in the world
Restrained

I can't be there to comfort you when you are sad
Can't be there when you are happy
I cause so much trouble
I am without answers
Why is a girl like you with me?
Why can't I give her what she deserves?
Am I living up to her expectations of her first?
Or have I failed?

I hate being restrained
Is it my fault?
Is she too perfect to be blamed?
Judgment will pass and forever my spirit will be gone
And maybe even her
Only time will tell

Forgive Me

I can't believe I said that
Those words that hurt you
Those words that I didn't mean to say
Those words that never should have come out
As they hurt you, you must also know
I was hurting too
What a fool I was
Now I can't help but wonder
Do you love me the same?
Or do you not love me anymore?
Questions that shouldn't be there
But they are

I can't believe it
I feel like a piece of dirt
As I sit here right now
All I can think of, is how could I?
Does she still love me?
I am so sad
It has been two bad days
Both just trying to let off steam
We figure that we will not stop loving each other
Still its no excuse for what I said
All I know is that I didn't mean a single word
Please forgive me

Missing

I missed you yesterday, today and probably tomorrow
What is missing you to me?
It's when I await your arrival
Letting the day pass quickly
Thinking of you every instant

It hurts too much
Missing your hugs
Knowing I can't get one
Missing your voice, touch, scent
Knowing they are not here

Waiting by the phone
Just in case
Ring...
But it's not you

I'm missing my half
I'm missing my love
I'm missing my angel
Missing your illuminating smile
Suffering but hiding it well
I'm gasping for air
Grabbing my pillow thinking it's you
And I ask, when will you come back
I'm missing you and it hurts so much
My heart is crying
Please come back
Precious queen of my heart
My love, please come back home

Nobody like You

I will never find anybody like you
Even if I travel through the whole world
Even if I live for a thousand years
There is only one of you

When you smile you light up my day
When you cry, it rains
Close to you I'm nervous
Far from you I feel empty

No other girl makes me feel this way
I feel that if I don't see you, I'll cease
If I don't talk to you, I'll go insane

There will never be anybody like you
Your flawless face, your splendor, your charisma, your attitude,
Your sweet lips, your caramel skin
Nobody like you
That phrase just sums it all up

My Truth

I want to tell how much I love you
But words are not enough
This Valentine's Day I want to go for the truth
The truth is I know
I know it's hard to be with me
I make you angry
I make you sad
I frustrate you
Please believe me that is not my intention
Even through all this time
I become nervous around you
I do not know how to behave around you
It's like falling in love with you again
Every kiss is our first
Each hug will not be the last
Your heart will forever be with mine
I do not mean to upset you
But I do mean to make it up to you
I mean to love you

Stage Four

"Years later...The Downfall"

I'm Sorry

I'm just trying to clear my head
I don't know if you even care
What I have to say or how I feel
Do you ever think about me anymore?
Do I ever creep across your mind?
What we had I wouldn't trade for anything
What we had everyone else just wished they had
We loved
Now we are just lost

I'm sorry you could not share your thoughts and feelings with me
I'm sorry you may not miss me anymore
I'm sorry you felt like I did not love you at times
I'm sorry I made you feel judged
I'm sorry you felt trapped
I'm sorry you felt you couldn't talk to me

Nothing to stop us but us
I could not hold us anymore
You just kept pulling away
You isolated me, kept me in the dark
You slowly dissected me out of your life
Like a man left in the sea of loneliness
Swimming towards the shores of love without hope

I'm sorry you broke my heart
I'm sorry that everything I gave was not enough
I'm sorry I was wrong about you
I'm sorry I gave so much
I'm sorry you cared so little

It could have been fixed
But I don't think I cared
Not a single tear was wasted
But the pain was still shattering
Like walking out of heaven

I'm sorry time did not stand still
I'm sorry you just stood still
I'm sorry I was used
I'm sorry this is how it had to end…

Two in the Same

I'm sad
But also glad
My heart is with pain
Yet my soul is filled with hope

A goodbye was said to my love
A love I grew to depend on
A love we both grew on
A rare flower in the garden of life
For this loss I am sad

The girl that lost it all
The champion of separation
The loser in the game of love
Hiding the ring I gave
Driving me to my early grave
The most materialistic person I've met
My love was not enough
A sad departure, but for this I'm glad

A relationship full of passion
When it came to love, it was an explosion
A long journey of good and bad
A love that withstood the test of time
A love envied by all
Now it's all gone

Freedom was the demand
No explanation was needed
She will miss me
She will hate you
Who was there on her lonely nights?
I was her company

When she was sad
I made her happy
When she was deserted
I stuck by her
I gave my life for her
Who will do that for her now?

I wish her the best
I wish you the worst
She was my sunrise and sunset
You are the cold in those long winter nights
I hope she finds her way back
Hope you lose your way
The problem still persists
You and she are one in the same
I love her and I hate you
Your dilemma is who you want to be.

How can I Forget (I Remember)

How to forget the forgotten?
How to remember to remember?

How can I not think about you?
You the first love of my life
The one that breathed life into me
The one that stopped the world from spinning
The one that gave my heart meaning
I still remember when we first met
The way we flirted
The day I asked you out
The movie we went to
The first time our lips touched
And the first gasp of air after that
How can I forget that?

The endless nights writing
The first grounding
The friday nights were ours
The first time I cancelled plans
The first time I heard your cries
That time we slow-danced
The parties and get-togethers
Homecoming and your blue dress
The first time we said I love you
I remember the first time we made love

I remember that light blue dress
A dress fit for my angel
The fights and disagreements
The make-ups and happiness
The first night we spent together
The first breakfast together
The cold walk that night
Your warmth that same night
Our first poor Valentine's Day
All challenges taken as a pair
Our love reached legendary status
A beacon for true loves

Time passed yet it stood still
From children to adults
I recall the pregnancy scare
I still feel those heavy tears of yours
The dancing lessons and the clubs
How can I be asked to forget it all?
The time apart we spent
The frequent miles traveled
I remember those dark days
The time we split
The instant we got back
The first night we loved again
That day at the zoo
Unforgettable that day was
Then time passed

I remember the proposal
Your tear-filled response
The ring my mother gave you
The ring I picked for you
Remember the lady that guessed our engagement?
The happiest moment in my life

I recall the change
I remember the fights
The last time we made love
The last time we said I love you
All but the last kiss
I still hear those last words
Everything from there is a blur
We were both wrong and proud
That was the day my world changed
That is the day I remember
How can I forget to remember the rest?
Do you?

Questions

So many questions to ask
To no one specific
Just to whoever answers
Help me understand the answers

Am I paying for something I did?
If I am, I regret whatever I did
Is this a test of my strength?
Please make it stop before I am spent

I had the world in my hands
I was the king of my world
Now the world crushes me with all its might
Now I am a peasant in this land now

Was this her plan?
To leave me in this land
Was I a toy until something came along?
Am I not good enough to love?

Is it because I loved so much?
Or is it that I made her my whole world?
She hurt me, so why do I suffer still?
Why can't she feel the pain I do right now?

She moves on, without looking back
I stay here, remembering the pain
How can she be happy so fast?
While I sometimes feel so depressed

So now I ask…
How did I get here?
Why did I change from a winner to a loser?
Please shed some light into my darkness

Just one more question
How long will this last?
One more question, I promise
Will I be happy again?

Snap

I sit here snapping my fingers
Listening to sounds of the past

Asking myself what went wrong
How did I get to this point?
Trying to forget the past and look to the future

I wanted to marry her
But she had something else in mind
I was so sure, where did I go wrong?
I know it was not me, it was her
And that is why I let her go
I still hurt, try to put on a show pretending I'm whole
So why do I suffer?

Don't get me wrong I loved her
But I'm hurt, my pride is gone
The man that once was is no more
I feel the wind cutting me
The faster I run away the harder it cuts
But I cannot stop, because she will not stop
I have to let it burn
The hole in my heart must close

It was said that once you close your heart for that person
It can not be opened again

I snap again
Music filling my soul

I do not know what to write
I don't know what to do
I know I have to move on

I must get to a point of peace
I thought she was for me
I guess I was mistaken
It feels like I was played into this position
I gave her everything I had
Yet I have nothing

A different song in mind, just snap I keep thinking to myself

I guess I will write what I feel
Women always complain about how there are few good men
That we are dogs
What I have come to realize is that the few good guys out there,
Die from the inside because of women like her
So do not complain, blame yourselves

Shhh, another song, just snap

Remember I was the one that gave you your first kiss
I still remember that
She will always be in my heart
I guess at the end a person just remembers the beginning
It all started so many years ago

Snap

Now I guess I'll take care of me
Why should I be sad if it was not my fault?
Why should I care, if she was the one that hurt me?
She should be thinking and being sad.
She broke us
Here is some glue, put it together
I thought she was the one once
But not anymore

Stage Five

"The Movement"

Letting Go

I know you are doing alright
But I wish you would ask me
I'm not going to lie
I still see you in my dreams
Once in a while you are in my thoughts
But it has to stop
I know I'm going to be okay

The damage is still here
Afraid to commit
Afraid to open my heart
My heart and soul are absent
At night my body shivers with loneliness
What can I do?

Letting go
To really let go, is to move on
If this is really your wish
Your last wish shall be granted
It's not fair to hold on
Let my heart be whole again
To let someone take care of me for once
Fill my nights with warmth
Let the past be

I guess it's true
You do not think of me anymore
The rumors of you are true
I must leave this alone
Move on and let this pass

Black Suit

The alarm brings me back to the moment at hand
Didn't get much sleep last night
Thinking about the love I had

Reminiscing what I'm going to forget
Thinking about all my regrets
Today,
A day full of sadness
This day of crying and pain

The day is so dark
I take a look at myself
Is that really me?
Unrecognizable to myself
The world seems to stop, trapping me
As I get ready I remember today
I remember why the black suit is next to me
For me, this is going to be a hard day

A day so dark
Without a shed of light
My soul so dark
Healer of wounds
My companion in this trip
Witness to the death of a dream
My friend is this lonely day
The black suit I wear today

I find myself in the shores of a birth
Where my knee touched the earth
To some the beach is calming
To me its aching
I smell the sea

I close my eyes and all I see is her
I heard the sea
But all I hear is her

I remember everything of her
What I don't remember is the last kiss
I gave myself; my all
I was the best man I could be
I guess it wasn't enough just being me
All that is left to do is break down
Cry for my lost love
My tears fill the sea
My weeping drains my soul
With each tear
I forget her
With each salty drop
Remembering I stop
The sea takes her away from me
The tear filled sea takes my pain away for me

Something whispering to me to stop
Telling me that my love is still alive
Something full of memories of her and me
My friend reminds me
The ring in my left pocket
Her ring, my mother's ring in my pocket
Four diamonds and a purple sapphire
That was the ring I gave to her
When I put that ring on her finger
I said forever to her
I guess forever for her came and went
Forgive me mother
But that ring to the sea it went
Her essence, our love, our dream
All gone with that ring

In this funeral no one spoke
Only one cried and it was me
But my suit comforted me
My black suit was the only one there beside me
The only one that accompanied me
The only witness to my downfall
Protected me from the downpour

Last tear on my surface
Ended the service
With my spirits lifted
I walk away
Leaving everything in the past
Me and my black suit
Leaving this place
Heading to a new horizon
My black suit and I

I wake up
I find myself in my room
It was all a dream
Its 6:30 am,
Saturday the 27th of October
And I remember her
The beach, the sea
All a bad dream
But looking at me
My black suit
Requesting me to live my dream
To stop remembering
To fulfill that dream
Asking me just to live again

Single

Go ahead raise your arms
Yes, you are single again
But don't kid yourself, rock star
Remember the game is open to me too

You were never a hunter
But the hunted
Be careful because I won't be there
Don't claim you are on the prowl again

Let your friends sway you again
We were a couple blessed by the stars
A beautiful thing, now wasted away
I was ready to give you my name
Now that mentality is gone

Saying I want you back
I guess spilling that drink on her was accidental
I guess all those hang-ups were just wrong numbers
The past is the past
So let it be

Be single again
I'll do that scene too
Looking for a lady to treat me well
No drama, just fun
Try to find another me
Yes, we are both single again
So enjoy
We can always be friends

Not a Story but Reality

Just an encounter
Not planned or premeditated
A simple hello
Simply some words and phrases
Instantly a connection
Unexpected, unexplainable, undeniable

A couple days later
Sharing thoughts like they weren't strangers
The deepest feelings spilling out
No fear of sharing everything

A feeling of comfort and peace
An obvious attraction
Relating over past loves
Seeking to handle this new era
What a beautiful thing, kindred spirits

Both so emotional
Both so humble and selfless
Both hurting, both recovering
Both not knowing what to do

This is not fiction but my reality
Now at the crossroads of this ordeal
Should I put myself out there?
Should I say anything?
Should I whisper my fears?

All I want is to ask her to take a chance on me
Tell her that I can take care of her
This magnetism, this connection is not a fluke
But a truth
Am I ready to leap?
Question is, will there be someone to catch me?

Maybe too soon, or is it too quick
Live the now not the later
Don't regret later what's in front of you now
I'm showing you sincerity
I hope you can see me with clarity

All I ask is a chance
Some time to try
A chance to continue this story
A chance for a never-ending story

Stage Six

"Rewind"

We Know

Look at us now
Who would have known?
If someone would have said this two years ago
Believed, I would have not
But it's reality
Writing our past
Knowing there is no us
Not being friends
Not even a mere hello
If only we knew

There was no last goodbye
No grand finale to our story
No last kiss given
No kiss to cherish
Not a cloud in the sky
One second there was a "we"
The next just an "I"

If we knew
We could have cherished every moment
Maybe more pictures of us
More nights of just talking
More moments of just us
I wish I would have loved you more
I wish we would have known
Now just sad regrets

If we knew
Would things have turned out differently?
Would we have tried harder?
Or just given up earlier?
Now all that is left is to wonder
I wish you well
I wish the bad memories erased
And the good to last
But now we know
Too late now

Lies

The truth shall set you free
But it was the lies that let me be free
Let me elaborate on this decree

Let me go back in time
Rewind to a dark time
It starts ten months ago
Same signs as two years ago
Same distaste for my presence
Same negligence for our essence
I remembered the missed calls
The mysterious calls on our dates
Shopping for outfits I didn't ever see

The lack of time she spent with me
The excuses to go out alone
And when I went; the feeling of urgency to get home
Picking on every defect or fault of mine
Couldn't say what I was thinking
Like walking in a mine field
Any misstep would not kill me but instead end us
But in killing us, it shattered me

Twisted inside
Confused on what to think, what to say
I did what any fool would do
Changed into a person I did not recognize
Paranoid and full of doubts
A fateful day two hours late she came around
Saying she was shopping for our night out
In her eyes the lies fed to me sank in
To her I was convinced
In reality I was already deceased
Sick of the lies told to me

I was there two hours ago when she got off
To New York & Company she went
That wasn't the only stop on the road
At the end a kiss seen a mile away
Sealing the deal her lies smacking me in the face
Are my senses failing me?
She was cheating on me
Ending our date early
But getting to bed at three

At this point everything spiraled down
We saw nothing of each other
We did not make love anymore
At least not with me
Creeping like I would not notice
Her lies opened my eyes
Breaking my heart at the same time
So I called an end to it
And with me the truth of it
A show was put on
Tears came down
Full of deceit and hypocrisy
That face did not last long
A new man arose

Miss her I guess
But the truth is here now
Why I cannot take her back in my life
The trust is gone
The love faded away
You see now the "she" is you
And you are her
Knowing all along of your filth
Now the truth has set me free
Imprisoning you with it

Do Not Read It

You should have told me
Straight and to the point
There was another
Only if you had the courage
It would have been better

Why were you trying to hide?
To save your already trashed reputation
Or to save him
We will get to him soon enough

Let me depict this further
This betrayal was planned from the start
I knew it from the start
The secret calls and messages
The late nights working
The evening gatherings
Yet I kept quiet

I wanted to see if you were good
If by chance the temptation would dissipate
But it just grew and grew
At the end you could not tell me the truth
Blank reasons were served
Why do you think we could not be friends?

I played along with your lies
Even made you think I wanted you back
No tear was shed though
Why waste a tear on a liar and cheater
Just a sad look back
Time wasted and a lesson learned

Now to the man in question
A man with no genuine decency
A man with superficial morals
A man so lost that only by sinking others will he surface

He first came to me with the mind games
Suggesting you were no woman at all
Signifying you were no good for me
His hot air just went up
Thought I was the weak one in this
So he went after you
And you fell into his plan

He told countless guys to sway you
Letting others do his job
Engagement didn't mean a thing
Giving you false advice
Pretending to be friends
All lies and deceptions

He was with another yet he wanted you
He even suggested breaking the engagement
Playing on your doubts
Trusting him for his ten years senior
What kind of person could trust this man?
I guess a person like you

You fell to the security trap
Instilled into you so many years ago
Why have real love?
If superficial love is so accommodating
You do not even love him
Just his money and security

Your relations are a secret
Ashamed of what people will say?
Or do you know it's just a sham
Your family does not consent
Your friends trust me more

You were right
I deserved better
And now he has you
What does that tell you?

Does he know you still think of me?
Do you know what he does at times?
Does he know he is just company?
Do you know you are just a trophy?

Judgment is not the purpose
Truth was the goal
In the end I am no one to judge
In the end I lost you
The truth is I won myself
So who is right or wrong?

All allegations will be denied
It is to be expected
This was not meant to see the light
But truth can only be in the dark so long

I do not mean to be hurtful
I just try to be honest
A concept I know it's hard to accept
The truth is what hurts the most
I apologize for the pain
Truth is a the plate I just served
Is there room for dessert?

Honestly, first I wanted to light a fire
Why taint the purity of fire?
Your stench will then spread
I wish you happiness in every form
Redemption comes from the heart
And now I see the truth:

You never made me laugh.

Maybe (Question)

It was a beautiful thing
A match blessed by the heavens
Then cursed from below
It vanished so abruptly

Two weeks from the event in question
A person posed a question
Would I take her back?
All I could say is maybe
A maybe leaning towards a yes

Three months after my hearts burial
Still with a sour taste on my mouth
Seeing her with another
But not the same one as a month ago
My friend brought up that same question
Yet somehow a maybe still resided

180 days passes
A beautiful girl on my side
Discussing the past to begin the future
That question came out from her mouth
The word "no" resonated from my lips
My mind whispered an "I don't know"

A year ago I was heartbroken
Now I can't complain
My heart mended
My love reborn
Waiting for me my love is
To see the sunset we go
I closed my front door
Turn around and I see her
Tears running down her cheeks
It was the forgotten one
Now that, that "maybe" is a definite "no"

Stage Seven

"Hope"

The Story

From strangers to acquaintances
From associations to relations
From relations to dust
That is the story

Blue green eyes with a touch of peace
That's what attracted me
From a simple hello
That ordinary day in the mall
To that eventful night
The first of many late nights

All those late night talks
Trying unsuccessfully not to fall
Trying not to give my all
Being my heart was not whole
A couple more dates
The hurt gone and my heart was whole again

Sharing the most intimate thoughts
During sunrises and sunsets we caught
From coast to coast
Knowing each other even more
A love so unexpected, so sudden
But not a single image was taken

Our hurried love was destined to be demised
My fears and doubts materialized
There was the age differential
And the family's disapproval
A woman like this I did not deserve
So a disappearing act was served

In my mind I see her sad face
Haunting me with that last kiss
A decision made of cowardice
Yet I wish her the best
Maybe one day I'll be ready
I hope that day comes soon

Can this be considered real?
If there is no proof you were really here?
The only proof is you and I
Until we cross again and tell the world

Fragrance

She is everything in my life
Loving everything about her
Her magnificent mind
Her gorgeous body
Even Aphrodite is with envy
Her soul and love
The way she loves me
But what drives me to insanity
What mesmerizes me is
Her fragrance

When her fragrance is recognized
My soul leaves me, to paradise
How is an angel with me I ask her?
She smiles and kisses me asking me why I am with her
I whisper to her that she loves me for me
That she is my better half
Even if she drives my senses to war
She, my Helen of Troy

Amongst them they fight
The second is blinded by her beauty
Number eight gets to hear an angel sing
The fifth gets to feel when I touch
Number nine tastes the strawberry on her lips
And the twelfth gets to play when we kiss
But all jealous of one

The sense of smell
Such a wonderful gift
Carried by cranial nerve number one
Foundation to the building called memory
The one that detects her fragrance
The first to tell me of her presence

Her hair bathed with fruits
Her caramel skin immersed in vanilla
All it takes is one scent to remember
The smell of fruits in my face
The aroma of vanilla on my skin
The smallest hint of berries on my lips
Remember the day she told me she loved me
Her fragrance in my bed calms me
Fruits and vanilla
The fragrance of the one that loves me
A fragrance I hope my nose forever detects

Love

Some say it's the butterflies
Some suggest it's at first sight
Some insist it's obtained with time
One thing is for sure
It's rare to find true love
The unconditional kind

When you love someone
It's not only attributes, but their flaws too
It's not only to know, but to understand
It's when one person puts the other first
Two people as one yet each their own

Love needs nourishment
A life source that needs to be provided
Love can withstand hurricane winds
But can also fall with a simple blow
To love is to help
Even if they do not call
To understand even when you do not

Love is not perfect
But the imperfections make it real
Be passionate about each other
Respect one another

It's the rarest love to find
Once recognized
Embrace it, fight for it
Unconditional love

Stage Eight

"Random Thoughts"

Forever

It is often said to last forever
But how long is forever?

Forever is to last to the end of a particular time
But each of our ends is a different time
This is not necessarily to the end of our lives
Just the end of that time
I will love you forever
But forever is really until when?
Until you leave or until you grow tired of me?

If a loved one tells you they love you and then adds the forever,
Don't take that as forever but as right now.
Maybe forever in memory
Forever cannot last forever
I may die tomorrow and my forever only lasted a day
A day is forever
But to us a day is just a day and time is our enemy.

If someone tells you they will love you forever
Take it, enjoy it, but don't be surprised when it ends.
Be surprised and rejoice when it does last.
Enjoy your love for as long as it lasts
You will remember it.
You will remember forever depending what your forever is,
A second, a minute, an hour, a week, a year- who really knows?
Only you can decide that.

Redemption

Every action has a reaction
Every choice has a consequence
Every bad deed doesn't go unpunished
The question is, do good deeds undo the bad?
Hope is what is left
Redemption is the choice
Hoping to lessen the chains carried
To save the soul from the clutches of damnation

The lies woven
The deceptions that were thrown
The friends lost
The enemies found

Forgive the ones that have done wrong
Appreciate the ones that love
Ask for forgiveness
Pray for their understanding

Young and naïve
Lost for years in a cloud of false
A shell of a person not there
Pretending to be whole
While losing the person that was

Live life honestly
Be true to yourself
Take each day as a gift
Cherish the loved ones
Maybe one day redemption will be found

Women

Women are the heart of the relationship
Without them men are alone
Women are the ones in charge
They ask, men give
Although they are in charge
They give men a say

A relationship is a partnership
A good partner knows the other's weaknesses
Listening to each other
Acknowledging people make mistakes and its okay
Follow each other's advice
Do not abuse the power
A guy may love you and you can be the greatest thing to
happen to him
But if too controlled, he will break loose

Women, be careful with a man's pride
If damaged the relationship will go sour
Do not be too serious, men are childish
Women, if you find a good man, fight to keep him
"Good men" are a dying breed
A good man is there for you
He may not know how to help you
Just tolerate him, don't hurt him

Do not think men are psychics
Do not think men actually know what's going on
If asked a question please answer
A good man gives what he receives
Trust me in the long run
It is worth it

It's Time

Throughout my life I have seen people kill themselves
It's a circle of vicious killing that never stops
It will stop only if we let go of our hate
It's not an eye for an eye
It's just a circle of destruction
Violence doesn't solve anything

I have seen people kill and hurt each other for too long
It's time to change
I have seen people's blood in the streets
Seen our babies homeless and hungry
It's time to unite
Together we will solve our problems
Violence and hate will get us nowhere
Apart we are being pushed around
Together we will be an unmovable force
We are all the same race and same species
Please let go of violent ways
It's time

Why do we hurt our women?
They are the mothers of our children
Why do we rape our women?
We should protect them, take care of them, and cherish our
precious resource
We should love them
Why do we leave our women with our babies all alone?
We should look after them
They are our future
Love them
Teach our babies to love and respect women
Teach them right from wrong
Raise them true

Without violence or hate
But with only love and caring
It's time to do it
It's time for humanity to be one

Happiness Shut

Happiness is the key of life
Where does it go when one is old?
Does it go or does it hide?
Does one block it?
Or is it simply lost

I am happiness
Where am I?
I am locked
I am still here
I will just have to wait
One will come and open this heart
Because I, happiness, will rise
If not, will this one live long?

Oh, why was I shut out?
Please let me out
Finally out
Who was responsible for this miracle?
Only but a child
Happiness thanks you, child
This person shall finally live
Life will be enjoyed
You just did the impossible
Thank you

A Moment of Silence

Is every life plotted?
Do you live long or are you allowed to live?
Are you in control of your life or is your destiny set?
Why does someone die so young?
A life full of light, full of fun
Is it fair to them or their families?

This young man is not done in life
He will never know what true love is
Will not experience graduation
First day of college
Marriage
Kids
All these great things he will not experience

Is it society's fault or are we at fault?
He didn't know he was going to die so young
He didn't ask to die
He didn't want to die
Did he deserve it?
Nobody deserves to die

All his life ahead of him, his hopes, dreams, goals, and ambitions
All gone with him
He could have made a difference in the world
But to all who knew him
He already made a difference
Whether he made you laugh, cry, upset, or even just a simple talk
Why was he called so soon?
I'm sure loved ones will miss him and mourn him
But all of us will ask "Why, why him?"
Why so young?
Why...?

Maybe he was too good for this world
Death is never easy and it will never be
So be thankful for life
And live life to its fullest
What if tomorrow never comes?
Well, it's not up to us
Let us pray he is in good hands
A moment of silence, please....

Eulogy

If death arrives tomorrow
What would be my legacy?
What would I say from beyond?
What would my loved ones do?

My eulogy and my goodbyes
I loved and was loved
I lived as best as I could
I had regrets and burdens
I had my secrets and truths
There was darkness in me as there was light

I was a son, a brother, a lover, and a friend
Most importantly, I was me
I was lost for a while
But at the end I was found

To those who hurt me
Forgiveness was passed long ago.
I thank you for the hurt
The pain inflicted made me stronger
If you did not love me alive
Don't mourn me when I'm dead

To my loved ones
Sorry I was taken so soon
Mourn that I'm not here
Rejoice the fact that I will always be here
I had aspirations and dreams
Be happy for what I accomplished during my time
Remember my qualities, not my flaws
But if my flaws are remembered, that just makes me real

All that I can ask is to be remembered.

After word

Love is enough to overcome everything if we let it, but as humans we are born with the fear to become overpowered with something we do not understand. Love is irrational so why try to rationalize it, just go with it and I promise the ride will be worth it. The darkness does not hold answers it just holds us back from getting them. Do not be afraid to love, be afraid of not loving.